THE POISON COLOUR

THE POISON COLOUR

poems

MAUREEN HYNES

Cover art Natasha Henderson, *Open Sonnet One*
Design Oberholtzer Design Inc., St John's NL
Typefaces Brioso, Helvetica Neue

Printed in Canada

Coach House Printing

Library and Archives Canada Cataloguing in Publication

Hynes, Maureen, author

The poison colour / Maureen Hynes.

Poems.

ISBN 978-1-897141-71-7 (pbk.)

I. Title.

PS8565.Y63P63 2015   C811.54   C2015-901300-3

Acknowledgements

The publisher wishes to thank the Canada Council for the Arts and
the NL Publishers Assistance Program for their generous support
of our publishing program.

for Ruth Kazdan

THE POISON COLOUR

FURTHER AND FURTHER WEST

CONDITIONS AT THE SURFACE

LISTENING TO THE GRASS

> When you got tired of walking
> you lay down in the grass.
> When you got up again, you could see for a moment where
>   you'd been,
> the grass was slick there, flattened out
> into the shape of a body. When you looked back later,
> it was as though you'd never been there at all.
> – Louise Glück, "Pastoral"

When you have tinnitus, everything
in the world – or in your head – sings a high-pitched
note that you learn to ignore; but when you
set about the business of *listening*,
the note gets higher, louder, unrestrained.
First you hear the grass singing – but that's your
own condition; then growling, chirping,
buzzing, churning. No – those are dogs, birds,
bugs, helicopters. What's the sound of air,
water, chlorophyll combining themselves
into sturdy green?

Stretch out, listen to the grass with your whole
body, not just your sandaled feet,
bristly mattress whose stuffing
scrapes your cheek, prickles your ear.
Now you hear the argument
among water, soil, *chepica* grass:
commotion of pale shoots as they dip
their new quills into Neruda's green ink,
deepen their hue and swarm ahead
three, six, eight inches, again and again,
all the way into the thirsty vineyard.

ELEMENTAL

Mark Rothko, *Untitled*, 1952
Tempera on paper, 101.9 x 68.7 cm
Collection Christopher Rothko

These are the elements that have sung me
through my life. A bar of blue, band of green, field
of terracotta; two ochre squares and three red
brushstrokes, surround of indigo. Template

for my childhood drawings – sky
and garden, roof and two windows.
Roundness not yet necessary, no people yet,
no ponies, cats or turtles. Just something standing,

smudged and breathing. These were the shapes
and colours unfolding as my flight landed
in this country: ocean and mountain, orchard and reservoir,
shopping mall and drive-in. And closer still,

from my window tonight, the sky ultramarine
over the burnt grass meadow, a derelict house
with two waiting windows, the vineyards
beyond. But always, reaching out to touch

the two ochre columns, their edges blurring.
Call them work and love, they support
the dark blue dreaming, sometimes peaceful,
sometimes quickened by three red lines.

THE SCIENCE OF TEARS

Today's article about tear ducts –
men's are larger than women's, but men
produce less prolactin, that complex hormone
of milk production and balance
of water and salt.

Larger storage tanks, but less cargo.

The world's fallen tears, anyone's tears,
turn into a mist over mountains and seas
and descend to the earth to form
the frost that crystallized
this morning

on the path's yellow leaves. The bitterest tears,
those of the orphaned and the disappeared,
drop deep into ocean beds, feed the living
stone of coral trunks and branches,
brighten them to a deep hibiscus red.

The way the earth sometimes cries –
inwardly, over millennia, its tears glistening
to a crusted beauty, a cone of sorrow in
darkened caves, taking the shape of our own
unshed tears: concealed, preserved.

CONDITIONS AT THE SURFACE

are inhospitable, so she drills into time,
        discovers a *Galapagos of the deep* –
vas-y, go ahead, the gold miners who died young
        don't mind as she bores
two point four kilometres under the town of Timmins
        through rock ice towards the magma core.
They know it's down there, more valuable than veins of ore.
        She collects a beaker of the ancient
musky-yellow water sealed beneath the granite
        two point seven billion years ago.
Half the age of the Earth. Sips the golden liquid,
        declares it super-salty to the taste, points
skyward to volcanic rock on Mars. We all look
        upwards – could be we share
the same deep water, *depending on conditions*
        at the time of entrapment.
She dips a quill into her glass beaker, notes every
        name she can think of – auroch, xenon,
pterodactyl, horsetail. Eon. She is trying to read
        this water's chemical signature
penned two point seven billion years ago.
        Billets doux. It's like finding another world,
she says. An other world.

the effect is blue, not periwinkle

But today four-petalled periwinkles appear
everywhere, now that I've swept away fallen
magnolia blossoms, brown-tipped, mouldering, and
whoa! splendid tree, twice
we've been hailed upon
in this northern spring, and still you flaunt
your crinolines. Across the street, an elderly man

gets off his bicycle to walk uphill
facing another *frente frio*, iceberg blue,
blowing in off the sea to wreak
ill-fitting panes from our window frames.
Some kind of voyage, from dread to sorrow,
from sorrow to resignation and back to
fear. I mean a passage from seeing

blue to tasting it, from listening to birdsong
to opening a jar of it. Who carries
its fragrance the furthest, which bird
scatters the cerulean seed to the ground?
Wouldn't you want to cross a field toward
your lover wearing a full-skirted dress printed all over
with that persistent flower?

earthquake

and so in this most welcome water season   the cracked
glass Phoenician vessel   glows coral in the dim light

of the stone musem's underground   in the coastal town
of Almuñecar   where salt was gathered

from the sea   dried in open vats
on the surrounding hills   olive groves and presses
to fill the amphorae with oil

                              I see the centuries streaming
like black water   their density barely recalled

                    most obvious

                                        complex of occasions
                    the human body

this occasion's intricacy   I recall my distant lover

how I move my hand   pour the oil   smoothing it upward

from her toes and ankles   over her thighs
towards her pudenda

                         (from the Latin *pudere,* to be ashamed)

Hera-like she emerges from her bath
her mound of Venus   hidden by the towel
held like a woven screen by two nymphs

her bathwater heated   by volcanic coals
like the lava beneath   the Haida Gwaii hot spring

but now cooled   by last October's earthquake
maybe loosening a single boulder to stopper

the earthcore's jagged fissure   buried beginnings
of the steaming hot springs   its rocky rim bordered

by salal and hellebore   with no warning
the bath chills   its heat source seized

                      stretch out my arms
to receive the woman

GESTURE

That was the night the dancer crouched
in stillness
down to her bare feet in the small pool of light,
picks of sparkle in the severe black hair that
fell over her face. The *mudra* of her hands
held the modern world and the ancient.
Then – slap of her feet against the ice-blue
glowing floor: how life and death burst out.
Eyes shining, she danced to morphemes,
to helicopter whirrs, the three bubbling notes
of a child's laugh, and the *khey, khey, khey*
of what is known and shouted. Fingers up
to the rafters, down to the earth and the grave beneath.
One by one, she discarded forty-eight
masks of desire, pain, distraction, to bare
the core of calm abiding. Her gesture of thanks at the end –
one finger's quick touch to the floor, then to her heart;
to floor, to forehead.

HUMMING

Luminescence: The Silver of Peru, Exhibit, Spring 2013
University College Gallery, University of Toronto

Could I drop
               the tunic over my shoulders,
cloak of six hundred silver squares
linked with silver wires? Hold my arms out
& let it fall ceremonially
over my breasts –

           thank you,
Peruvian silversmiths, for the burden
of your thousand-year-old mantle which is now
healing my heart & breasts & lungs,

             for the weight of your rayed monstrance
as I raise it priest-like above my head;
             for the medicinal scent
of your silverwork armadillo pomander.
                 Undetected
by guards I lift out of the glass case
your necklace of nine hummingbirds.

             Their blackened beaks are closed
needle points I tease open with my thumbnail, find in each
a seed from the Tree of Wisdom.

            There is no clasp. The birds perch
on invisible molecular strings – their mid-air nectar search
so like kissing,
        a Hesitation Tango they dance
down ten centuries.

Necklaced, my throatpulse polishes silver into song,

        warms tarnished wings into glint and thrum.

JEWEL BEETLE DRESS

John Singer Sargent, *Ellen Terry as Lady Macbeth*, 1889
oil on canvas, 221 x 141.3 cm

Lady Macbeth lifts the golden round:
breath held, sexing herself
with the crown. Arms pale.
Magenta braids down to her knees,
two loops of woven gold
around her waist and hips.
A spilling dress of blues and greens
adorned with jewel beetles –
iridescent asterisks
stitched up and down.

                As if the only way
to display her brilliance is to costume her
in carapaces – not gems from Persia
but these creatures that follow pine smoke
to lay their eggs in burned-out forests.

This week a dead grasshopper appears
in my watercress, pale green body
hinged and folded
like a child's penknife – with eyes.
And here, and here, fascination

with the dress: could I sew one,
a basket of dead beetles at my side,
pushing the needle through those bodies
over and over again? Could I wear it –
the beetles' weight scattered along the folds,
over my breasts and down my back,
on the glint-edged sleeves
that graze the floor, taking
power from these jewels
to speak remorseless lines?

TORTOISESHELL

To bring the night sky to life,
strike a wrong note from time to time
– Charles Wright, "Wrong Notes"

Like a daily haze, the drumming lesson
spread through the old city. Sixty clanging minutes
reverberating at day's end
on brick wall and cobbled road,
spire and cypress tree; it seemed to have
no source and every source. *How can people
live with this,* I cried.

Later we found the drumming student
and his teacher in the empty market. Tortoiseshell,
the citizens call the open-air structure,
for its ovaloid roof, Siena-tiled,
held aloft by pillars. Perfect echo chamber
pitched in the city's core.

Pray for the pauses to elongate. Saint Catherine –
another miracle. Grant the child some musicality
and rhythm. Mercy for the voiceless tortoise,
spare its aged heart and sturdy shell.

MAILBOX

All night my dreams snowed letters. Singly
and in sheaves, tissue-thin airmails
fell into my hands. Pages folded and signed,
some with Chinese script and Chinese stamps.
On red stationery inside a red envelope,
a shout of congratulations.

And me carrying armfuls to the mailbox.
Waking, I wondered at this avalanche
of correspondence. Mid-day I found my forgotten
letter to you in the bottom of my pack, stamped
and addressed, promises

to visit next spring. And now the call
from your wife – your stroke,
your memorial. Ah, god, Michael,
which is worse, a farewell or none at all?

SMALL CONTAINERS

Always finding in my morning walks
the scraps and shards of *before* –
cramped cul-de-sacs and elbow turns
like Jersey Ave with garages like broken teeth
opposite workers' cottages –
the street where my grandparents made
their first home.

Broad boulevards now tawdry and commercial
stretch back two hundred years,
home to doctors and merchants
and clergymen. The same cathedral bells
chime the hours, quarter, half and full.
How long does it take a city
to form us, fill us
with longings shaped before we were born?

Here and there, nearly concealed,
a Green Man molded in red clay frowns
from two or three storeys above – moustached
with leaves and branches, vines, verdure
for hair, eyebrows, beard. Ghost flares,
a compositor or milliner, accountant or seamstress,
darting across the windowframe–
a minute's stolen break.

Silhouette of the old brick city
etched each spring in ivy branches
up a library wall. July afternoons
around Casa Loma, mulberry-stained

sidewalks where my father gleaned the tart fruit.
Lanes now named Milky Way or Dragon Alley
lined in summer with hollyhocks and milkweed –
then iced over in winter, two jagged wheel ruts.

The Spadina theatre shut down by Red Squad cops.
A necklace of factories at lake's edge –
sugar refineries, tanneries, distilleries, rolling mills.
Silos for wheat and wharves now speckled
with cargo crates and docking kayakers.
Tiny owls nesting on Leslie Street Spit.
The lake under the lake.

Living the whole city, absorbing it
corner by corner, year by year,
holding it within until
we turn our bodies into small containers
for the places where we come to consciousness.

POLICEMAN

What'r you doing in that dress,
a policeman said.
– Lorine Niedecker, "Depression Years"

This iris sheath
furred with moss lined with a hiss
a kiss of silvery
olive leaves, put on in honour
of the day my sister married
in a schoolhouse chapel. I stood
high-heeled, bouffant hair, mauve
chiffon: distant war preying on my mind.
My mother in a cornflower dress,
flaxen-petalled and honey-winged,
an outfit sewn for her in the Troubles,
the middle part of her life.

That was another decade you missed,
I told my grandfather
when I got over my surprise, finding
his face in a Queen Street gallery.
Wide framed group photo, 1941.
What'r you doing in that dress, I asked him,
police cap and folded hands and prominent chin?
You in a home uniform, dead ten years later,
and me in the family duress. I mean dress.

PLY

Block-printed in black ink on the back of a storage unit
built for me: a paragraph of praise to the Mosquito aircraft,
fighter bomber made of five-ply birch. "Scrap ply," he writes,
splintering me into sudden sorrow.

After the war he scrounged discarded bits, old motors,
Air Force plywood for household plans. Fast and light,
the Mosquito could do two sorties in one night (ash
from bombed-out buildings pluming to the stars). Seven thousand

built, none still flying: twentieth century labour
and its aluminum, circuit wire, Bakelite, parachute silk.
The utilitarian unbeauty of the things he made,
their essential modernity and jim-jammery. Tenderness

for copper wires and rubber plugs, the layers of his life.
Powerful little airplane, wooden wonder whose wings
were *ironed* into shape, stinging me now, asking why
didn't we think to commission a scrap ply casket for him –

a loving frugal use of one material for two things.

GWEEDORE, 1830s (BONFIRE)

The village teacher's inventory
from the parish of Gweedore, Donegal
in the decade before the Famine,
record of the belongings of four thousand people –

> 1 cart, no coach or any other vehicle, 1 plough
> 20 shovels, 32 rakes, 7 table forks, 95 chairs, 243 stools
> 2 feather beds, 8 chaff beds, 3 turkeys, 27 geese, no bonnet
> no clock, 3 watches, no looking glass above 3d. in price,
> and no more than 10 square feet of glass

Gweedore, just up the road from Gortahork. Heartland of Irish speakers.
Is it possible no knives? A seaside community, no curraghs or coracles?
Consider
ten beds and seven forks
for four thousand people and *no clock*.

Both towns in the shadow
of Mount Errigal, *Earagail* in Gaelic, on whose plateaus
fifteen-year-olds gathered around bonfires
the night before they emigrated.
No bonnet. No work, no food, no land.

My own count: no cart or coach or any vehicle, no plough,
but a shovel and a rake. The new BBQ from Canadian Tire. Twelve
wooden chairs and twelve folding chairs, three tables and two beds,
44 knives, forks, spoons. Two sofas and a coffee table.
A kilometre of books.
A clock in every room. 3 watches, yes, on my dresser.
Mirrors galore and a closetful of clothes and boots. No bonnet.

Brimful, sickened by surfeit.
Those earthen-floored bedless, bookless homes –
how full their heads and hearts?
The plentiful prayers of the coachless faithful.

OVERTIME IN THE SCRIPTORIUM

She smoothes out calfskin vellum
sets pots of verdigris
red and yellow ochre   in reach

lapis   gold powder   silver leaf
the first black letters   in a folio
of tall script   turf fire smoking her page

but her fingers   never warm enough
a lifetime on a high stool
at a sloped table   outside margins

of illumination and inside knots
of hunger   she writes   tower
blackbird   sand dune and fever

sleep   she writes in an alphabet of trees
snakes her letters   into saints and insects
lightning   magpie

coils her Latin into animals
and open-mouthed fish
traces a rusty path   out her winter window

the empty stool beside her

A THOUSAND STONES

PLAZA DE PUERTO DE MOROS

They are like flames or waves, the mesmer-tricks
        of the *golondrinas*, swallows, comet-tailing
above the Plaza de Puerto de Moros, the Moorish gate

in the old city wall. Like fire the birds seem never to rest,
        stitching market roof to cathedral spire to cypress crown,
looping the gathered up over the horizon

        into constellations. Taste their calls,
how their wings soften the air.
        Darling, I said, over almonds and olives and Spanish beer,

their spinning and darting reminds me of love
        moving the parts of our bodies without sound.
Solitary in flight but never alone,

the swallows are threading their lives together.

RESTORATION

"Gather a thousand small stones from a driveway, say,
or a gravel pit; place them in a bowl, the bowl
inside your front door. Each stone a week of your
remaining life. Every seven days, drop one to the driveway
or garden, or from an overpass to the railway tracks."

The teacher notes her students' discomfort: they want
to turn the exercise inside out, to *collect* a stone each week.
Start with zero and go to full. Understandable reluctance –
it's like sleeping in your coffin, or propping it open-lidded
against your mantel. That reminder to count the thousand

absent blessings, finger them like flinty beads. My mother's
Pyrex bowl, its chipped blue rim and its slow emptying,
life's stone soup evaporating at my threshold.
But still a grain of sweetness in that invitation
to restore what I have borrowed to the world.

KINDLY STOPS

Osorno, Chile

The car of love crawled into the rundown part of town,
past the *Ropa Americana* thrift shop and earthquake-
damaged stores, their wooden balconies awry,
Te amo, Te amo, Te amo – o – o – o – o – o – o
in magic marker scrawl along its sides,
coughed to a stop beside the old stone fort
and stretched out its wings, its doors,
to let the newlyweds out. The way they signalled
each turret, north south east west, with a kiss
got me missing you.

When I arrive home, you say
my long absence awoke a fear –
sleek black car with chariot wheels and obsidian
wings, panther face in chrome on the grille.
When might it pounce into our driveway,
who would be first snatched
into the passenger seat, who
left behind to watch.

POEM CALLED 'GRATEFUL'

after Joanne Kyger's 'Grateful', in About Now: Collected Poems

Could you write one, too? Book a couple of months
     in the Gran Hotel de Gratitud in Mérida,
spend it changing anger to peace, calm,
     forgiveness, repair? Fill the city's harbour with
appreciation, undo every kind of harm in the streets.
     Journey westward to Pátzcuaro, grateful
for the lives but not the deaths of 43 students, their parents'
     anguish, and the president barely held to account.
You could fling your fury into any old river, the Humber
     or Seine, the Shannon or all 246 rivers of Mexico.
Run rage under every shiny bridge whose alchemy
     can turn contamination into sweet medicine
for every living creature, *all of us waiting for gratitude.*
     Rivers have been given worse, as have mountains.
That day in September so thankful to pay
     a brief Yom Kippur visit to a city ravine,
throw the year's stones into Taylor Creek.
     A glorious sunny morning, a release,
like slipping into a *long forever nap of true sleep,*
     as if a few stones would rid us
of the evils we've done, the evils we've permitted.

ADAR

I cast a prayer down like a good old Catholic
to summon Adar, the additional month, the pregnant month
month of good fortune for Jewish people
that promises constancy in flux –
Adar's secret: *the end is wedged into the beginning*

this morning in the synagogue two women
slide open the gilt doors
reveal the six Torahs   brocade-cloaked cylinders
a girl of thirteen carries the heavy
scripture up and down the aisles
the scroll is unwound
men with small boxes of Torah verses
strapped onto their foreheads
pressing the holy words into their minds
bare arms bound

light falling through stained glass tints the faithful

the girl reads aloud the Hebrew
but the language is not fully unlocked
women still not permitted to pray at the wall

as we wait for the month of laughter to begin
I cast down the question
who can approach the deity

this unworthiness
no matter the religion

For a single strand

O little arachnids, the silk you spin for webbing,
wrapping prey and cocooning eggs: we've taken
your weightless scaffolds, your gluey guy wires
and kitestrings that carry wingless spiderlings afield
where the spinning begins anew;
we've stolen your industry, *stronger than*
steel or Kevlar, enduring bites and stings,
knotted it into nets to catch minnows,
spread it on wounds to knit them closed,
made the finest crosshairs
for microscopes and rifles.

O Golden Orb spider with your eight striped legs –
for your marigold silk, whose gleams
stitch tree to Madagascar tree, eighty collectors
with swollen hands gather a million
stinging females, pilfer filaments
to make just one thread, those sharp-eyed spinners
braiding ninety-six sunlit lengths. For four years
twenty weavers work at golden looms

to turn your silk into unsurpassing brilliance,
museum cloth no human will ever wear.
A sign of love's lightness, its tensile strength,
for a single strand to give to my lover
I'll trade you a Lorca poem in sunflower ink,
an Arctic sky, my city street's melting snow.

QUIPU

Museum of Precolumbian Art, Santiago, Chile

Looped onto the museum's woven canvas
a large swirl of string, curve of a pelican at rest,
its bill tucked into its chest. Glassed in,
bursting out to the frame, the circle emanates
ray upon ray, a fling of water
from a dog's back, string flecked with
beige, black, grey, brown knots.

Imperial accountants – Inca bureaucrats –
tallied the empire's taxes in llama yarn knots,
recorded supplies and merchants and exports.
The *quipu* – a kind of woolen abacus, ancient.

But missing is the work of their colleagues,
those who tied tales and poetry onto cords.
Would cochineal red or shell-pink string
mark the song of sisters who founded
warring families by falling in love with twin brothers?
Or yellow knots on green string for a century
of springtimes? Where is the black tangle for
flashfloods down the Andean hillsides
that washed out settlements or
thick browns for years and years of drought?

Marvellous system, but what comes back
is my grandmother fingering her beads, five sets of ten
she called *decades* before I'd heard of years.
Decades to recall the annunciation, the crown
of thorns, the resurrection. She used to say
she was *telling the beads* – revisiting
a story with each one, her Catholic knots.

THESE PERSONS

When I walk these city streets with others, when I tour
through seasons of scarcity past the faintest
scratched out remainders, the lost architecture
that the polis subtracts, when I stamp my feet
in the schoolyard at the end of my old street to summon
the riverside Native villagers underfoot or when
I point three stories up to the faded sign for a furrier's shop
or to wide warehouse windows
where immigrant garment workers stitched and a few
still stitch, or, on the red brick building on King Street,
to the enamelled sign for a short-lived
newspaper with socialist leanings, when I pass the
church whose Depression era faithful occupied
homes in defence of those evicted, when I search
for old names carved into stonework
or when the peepshow of the past reveals a woman
in high heels dashing into the bank that was once
the Victory Burlesque, all these sites
the city has buried or bricked over or overlooked,
then I am thinking Olson's thought,
My problem is to make you believe these persons existed

VALPARAISO

1. *Historia*
From the clouds, a young woman
dropped her enormous fishing net
over the forty-two hills; she traced
the net's splits and wandering lines
with a fountain pen the size of a young monkey tree.
Where the splits were biggest she put plazas
and the rest of the diamonds and zigzags
etched a jumble of steep narrow streets.
Forty generations and she's still at it,
scribbling between the Andes and the Pacific.

2. *Colores*
What about the ocean brings out
the harlequin in us? Are these crayon colours
a costume? Or the young woman's gift to warm
our cliffside homes, take our minds off
poverty and rain?
The orange and turquoise and lime green
of St John's, the Algarve, Valparaiso:
how we keep the sunset all day, fluorescence
of the tossed-up starfish all winter, store up its memory
against the blending of sea and sky into one grey slate.

3. *Sabor*
The sacramental wine leaves a taste
in the mouth, pewter or the heavy hinges
on the cathedral's wooden doors
or the star-laden Atacama sands blowing in.
Before her journeys, she gathered

a portful of salt, spread a tablecloth
the colour of cornmeal; then abandoned
her lemons and limes, her chilies and tomatoes.
Volcanic ash and the failure of another coastal fishery
stirred grit into her rice.

4. *Musica*
A lunchtime balladeer moves from table to table, singing
about the lovers on the port's stone walls, knotting
and unknotting their promises. Climb up to La Sebastiana
past the aerosol art and Manga graffiti, the radio concerts
floating from curtained windows, to the plaza where
we hum the songs of dead poets, chant
Spanish subjunctives to the young woman
(*Would that I were not so lazy*). Take refuge
in the cloud chair, sip our black tea and drift
in the music of the Americas, into the past, the future
or the blessed faraway.

STONE SONNET

You could pour a cathedral, a Stonehenge or a Gaudí,
into the Don Valley beside the straightened
waterway, dismiss the stonecutters, master
craftsmen that they are, and tip thick sandy liquid
into soft bud-shaped spires held in place with
rebar straws. You could light a long-burning fire,
melt silica and lapis and veins of copper verdigris
into sheets of azure or ruby or leafgreen glass
to lighten a temple or mosque or synagogue,
then climb the scaffold and chisel a fish
over each arched doorway, just to recall
the flatfish on the inmost wall
of the Paleolithic cave, that ancient home now slowly
emptied of images by our breathing presence.

CORMORANT ELEGY

The cormorant in the panelled hallway off the dining room
breathed quietly; he took the form of an old black
telephone, rotary dial. Beside me at the seder table,
a friend slid her hand over mine with each mention
of loss in the Haggadah. We passed words around
with bitter herbs, shankbone and roasted egg,
everything unleavened, broken, to mark the suffering.
All through the meal, waiting for the phone to ring,
I stiffened at the cormorant's moans. When he lifted
his head or stretched out his wings, an ICU reading:
your skin an eerie orange, messages of your organs
failing one by one. And now, this spring, every Passover,
though daylight lengthens its promise and the moon
rises again, the black-cloaked seabird shifts in the hall.

WING ON

for James Schuyler

What pebbles to set on your tomb
hold all through your jazz memorial

in the Wing On funeral home
A row of bluets to stain the stone

Just one greasy lipstick kiss on your granite
in a ruby shade called *Willing*

not smeared as on Oscar Wilde's marble tomb
Place delphinium feathers and Noxzema jars

pill bottles filled with catalogue seeds
a tiny plastic boat to swim out to

It's pink-shirted teenagers' day up the street
Honk for Equal Love they wave

Let's flashmob the grotto at Lourdes
Let's fishnet the legs of all the girls

Amaryllis, hyacinth, every shade of rosehip
a *cross-stitched border of spruce and juniper*

Throw a few coins into the busker's cup
Buy the poet a meal

Why don't we take a yellow song, carefree
and refined, put it on a long stem and stand it

in a skinny crystal vase? Add a pair
of topsiders to wear on the little boat

REDHEAD

Cornell Lab of Ornithology recording of Aythya Americana,
Redhead Duck, Minnedosa, Manitoba, 3 May 1961

lifting & tossing a long throw of *weee-ooo*
                                            marsh-distance away
baby this shrill, keep it throatal & safe
unhoneyed
perpetuate the trill

this is what an early May morning is
        just this
floating idle exclamations across the cool grey air
                losing or gaining energy from the calling   who cares

a flutter of recognition

                        flotation & bobbing
how can you get close enough?
the pierce/piece in an edge of reed-knit water-ring
what machine *splees* like this

fade to baritone & utter a splash

slicing through water as easily as air
cold or bright   blue or grey
zipper into the fright of it

just stay in this basket of sound

THE POISON COLOUR

après vous

after a talk by Donna Orange

about the suffering stranger & the wise baby,
the reach of kindness scorned. onstage
in the lecture hall a bouquet of 36 white roses.
we remember *the terrible silence*
& those swallowed into it. *the war goes on,*
wrote James Schuyler in 1972.

      meaning is external, she says, it comes in search of us.
a sentence i carry around the rest of the week.
once tortured, always tortured & i remember
the man in power whose father gave him
a lie detector test. my kindness fails, i cannot
extend it to him,
              nor would it soothe him. someone asks
why our kindness embarrasses us. i count candles & cards,
calls & cavities as one year rounds into another.
several times i shut my eyes to wars & fracking,
things that distress me, the deep scars
on the saleswoman's inner wrist.
                 i warm a marble
mortar & pestle, grind chilies & peppers, cumin & mustard seed
into a fragrant haze. she talks more about kindness, loving
kindness, the kind that abundantly pours.
                    after our departure
the petals of the 36 roses (i had mistaken them for yellow)
would fall on the floor. non-indifference, she calls it,
that disposition of *après vous*, always putting the other first.

poetry is a virus, said the Icelandic writer –
each generation of teenagers catches it.

TENDRILS

Siccative, the air: cracking and flaking everything – soil, the paint on the truck, every kind of bark

The geometry of the vineyards: no matter where I stand, a perfect row stretches star-like to the horizon from the centre

The heft of rough soil – O, Seamus, you swallow my experience whole. I fit my hand against a small mound of dry earth, its cracks match the lines on my palm

Clusters of unripe grapes like small green pellets in my hand

You, old woman vine, supported by stick and wire

And the stalk of this young one, barred like the neck of a guitar

Above me, oddments of bird chirp

A pool of water the size of a wooden wheel, its rim glistening. Nearby, a nest on the ground, a circular twining of yellowed grasses. A clock of thistle, like an artichoke, face down in the mud

In the next row, the exquisite datura. Pulling one leaf through my fingers imparts a deadly chemical scent on my hands. O Georgia, can I do you justice? Whorling white petals at their tips, each wrapping around the next. Small embraces, loosening

Thick rusted pipe like a ship's vent protruding from the ground – Persephone's telephone, she's below for the winter, trying to reach us

ARS POETICA, FILM NOIR VERSION

You book yourself into the Terminus Hotel,
three days' journey by ship and rail.
You borrow Magdalena's satin dressing gown,
she offers a gardenia which you wear

on your wrist like a fragrant watch.
You stand at the ship's railing while bystanders,
buildings, the shoreline disappear.
A bearded young man behind you

is singing a ballad in Esperanto –
beautiful, almost intelligible.
You have packed letters and poems and
the book about lesser known women artists,

a single feather and the eucalyptus pod twisted from its branch.
Before your destination, all must be incinerated
in the ship's furnace: the words, the song,
the gardenia, even the gown – fuel to carry you forward.

THE POISON COLOUR

In the Knit-o-matic store
a skein of Japanese wool; the saleswoman
shows me a knitted-up square –
Mexican tapestries, wild sunsets
in the south of France, mustard fields
ripening into full bloom –

her finger on a brown strand, says
They put a poison colour in each batch:
one colour that doesn't match. So much
poison in the world, and here is a use
for it, in socks and toques and trailing scarves.

To circle round in every group and wonder:
who is the poison colour here? The one whose dullness
makes the rest of the group brighten?
The colour so drab it intensifies
the merriment in all the others,
their alacrity and charm.
                              Is it me?

Take five pretty colours,
like five slender sisters, and add a sixth,
the prickly less-loved one who makes the others
sweet and tractable,
who forces their brilliance and grace.
The poison is not in the colour, nor in the huge brass
vats sunk into the ground, the cones of powdered dye;
not in the boiling water that releases the indigo,
sumac scarlet, turmeric yellow. It's inherited

like skinny feet or weak eyes,
a thread that runs through them all.

MOTHWING

My friend Steven showed me a photo of D. D. Ryan's "mothwing"
 eyebrows because James Schuyler had mentioned them
in a poem, and yes, resemblance to the large dusky moth that,
 wings outspread, died beneath my porch light.
In my youth, I despaired of having beautiful
 eyebrows rather than sparse ones. We need not mention
anyone's third eye or Ash Wednesday smudges or consider
 Frida's brows although her photo
hangs above my computer – aproned and full-skirted, pensive,
 smoking, she is sitting on a stool, leaning back
against her bookcase, that line of untended hedge
 between her eyes, that fine arc above her upper lip.
An old telephone beside her on the wall, its two round metal bells,
 and a receiver that hangs on a hook; sometimes I call her up,
tell her in my best Spanish that if I could order eyebrows
 from the dispensary I would ask for cedillas. Or green samaras
from maple trees in spring. The curve of a tulip stem three days in a vase.
 Or two new moons to suggest a distant benevolence.

ANDALUSIAN PIANOS

In the three Lorca houses the troubling silence
of the pianos, two uprights and one grand, shawled.

Outside, tassels of purple wisteria dangle
from balcony railings to the gravel path.

Brass sconces affixed, their candles
unlit for years, each piano lid closed,

no sheet music on the stands. The oil portrait of Isabel
at the keyboard, her trimmed fingernails, gaze intense.

In the dining rooms, art deco leather chairs and lustreware
on cabinet shelves. Tiny elegant cups, gold-rimmed.

Pussy willows in a black vase on a starched
white doily. Two dried red roses

on a notebook, two on the bed. On a ledge
behind a bedroom curtain, his broken-stringed guitar.

In each house, a chill rising from immaculate ceramic floors.

HOLY WEEK

We have had Semana Santa, we have had the Hallelujahs,
in Andalucia we have stood well aside
for the *toro de alleluias* running the cobbled streets.
Metres of red brocade woven
through balcony spindles, below us
processions of penitents, frightening
in cone-headed masks. These pageants
that Lorca denounced – *commercialism*, he said,
that buries the Muslim and Jewish and Gitano
roots of life and profanes the Alhambra. Earlier,
the dark night of the Gethsemane soul and the fourteen
stations of betrayal, the moral and monetary traitors:
we have stuffed newspapers into T-shirts and jeans
and skirts to make male and female
effigies, *quemas de Judas*, hung them from railings,
burned them. A young man with saffron-tinted
wounds in his abalone hands and a crown of thorns
has carried the splintering cross up Sacromonte hill,
the pomegranate tree from which it was planed,
its bloody seeds a tonic for the throat and heart.
We have unwrapped cellophane from the carved
Paschal candle and at midnight set off fireworks
for the year's long nights. We have entered
the sepulchre with its drawings of horses
and fish in ochre and coal, blood and fire.

CUEVA DE PILETA

Benaoján, Andalucia, Spain

1.

Animals have spoken but only the crows have decorated.
I didn't know I would be drawn into a living being – circuitous,
every surface slippery moist. That I could stand
inside a cave and feel it breathing.
How does the impulse to draw something begin?
Charcoal was our first pencil; iron oxide mixed with melted fat our first
    paint.

2.

Many chambers, steep passageways, drapes of calcium carbonate dyed
    green
with copper, purple with magnesium oxide, five storeys high. *Chimineas*,
    hearths with ventilation upward to the open air, black with
    millennial fires.
Everywhere, drip of stalactites, slow accretion of stalagmites, some
    broken by *terremotos*.
Five thousand bats: the single ring of a cell phone will wing them outside.
Their guano drew the olive farmer inside – his grandson guides us.
Breathe in. Sideways through a narrow passage into a home
with paintings 29,000 years old. A fish as big as my outstretched arms.
Goats, aurochs, so many horses; the famous pregnant mare – the
    dropping curve
of her belly that I want to stroke. Stick figure with a bow. V-shape
with emanating rays: *fertility symbol*, says the guide.
Calendar markings, a row of seventy downward strokes, a single line atop
joining them all: the most recent four thousand years old.
Down a closed-off corridor, two hands outlined with blow-paint.
Don't touch.
Shards and bones, animal and human, at its mouth.
I would sit in this damp cavern, draw my knees up to my chest,
rest and dwell and die a little here.

3.
Iron gate, now barred and chained, padlocked at the cave's mouth,
aching knee that lifted me up lowers me down the uneven steps
cut into the hillside. All of us,
prehistorics and ancients and *contemporains*, with or without medicines,
picking our way over stony paths, through hemispheres,
hauling firewood and giving birth, fishing and cooking, climbing steep hills
to winter in caves. Most of us in pain, pushing on.

4.
Afterwards, the train ride back through scrub and forest and jagged
outcropped mountains. The soil bleaches on both sides of a river,
reddens again. A herder grazes his brown goats
between train tracks and industrial blocks. Palm trees. A dog curls up,
goes to sleep in the sun. Three squadrons in desert fatigues and laden packs
quick-march down a road. O you young men. Four horses in a hot field,
     three black
and the white one shaking its head. A rabbit bounds
across the red earth into an olive grove, white tail showing.

RATTLE

There's a new rattle in the wind, a new texture to what blows.
Spinifex bushes dot the outback's blowing sand,
its slopes and hollows. Sifted into red sandstorm dust:

gum wrappers, foil bags, plastic water bottles,
empty tinnies. In the old days, says the Uluru guide, the desert
and its people were self-sufficient – what they discarded

enriched the land. A second Gonwanda emerges, the mid-
Pacific Gyre's garbage patch, mirror to the four thousand pieces
of space flotsam hurtling through the stars. Daily I trouble myself

with the household's petty excess, jam jars and junk mail,
a bag from every airport. I carry twenty unmatched
lids and eight containers to the bin, the half-life of glass

nearing that of plutonium. Why not create something of value
with all this carboniferous energy? Simplicity and care.
And our bodies, what of them, now and after death?

Yesterday a thick grey cloudbank was towed across
the evening sky by a thousand invisible strongmen hauling
in a snowstorm, obscuring the sunset, the endless ceiling of night.

SURGERY SUITE

Ninth floor
I want to be bandaged like this forever,
immobilized, panning to the lake through
drug-slowed eyes. From here
I'll cast my weighted net,
dredge up the shell of an old love,

a handful of baby teeth, willow leaves,
smooth shards of soupbowls and snuff bottles,
pull them all under my twisted sheets
to cool me through the drenching night.

66 slices
Manage your own pain, don't
bother the nurses. Ten hours
after joint surgery, the anaesthetic suddenly
wears off. To listen to your body
before it speaks, harder than you think.
The middle of the night.
I can bear it, you tell the nurse,
but I just can't stop crying. Push

the pain pump's middle button.
The apparatus clicks and clacks –
someone inside, very old and expert, is preparing
your dose, cutting slivers from a ball
of black opium. The sound of his scalpel
slicing against a porcelain plate.
In the middle of the night
you count: 66 slices.

Sleepwalk
Pain keeps the lamp on:
hard to fall asleep, stay under. A shallow,
placeless sleep to which the drugs
deliver you, an early dawn
that you've been jetlagged into. Wide-eyed.
An overnight flight that takes you close
to the casualties of chemotherapy,
road accidents, car bombs. Not to mention
their families, onlookers.
Somewhere
someone else is alert. A new knee
to sleepwalk down the years with.
Get your mind to match
the body's resolve. Watch
the deepest cuts knit together,
a stocking of bruises
gartered up your entire leg
oh-so-slowly disappearing. Recovery
is possible. What the body wants,
what the skin is teaching you.
But, for the moment,
this pain

AFLAME

Whatever it takes, she says. Sunspilled bedrock
burns the soles of her feet. Chemical
fire has set her hair aflame, scorched it
to the roots. The luminous photo of the back of her head –
just a scattering of slender dark hairs.

But hospital research is underway
for a salve to tickle follicles and the hair buds within.
Apply a stethoscope to her scalp, listen for chuckling.
Her crowning story. She's humming *Walking After Midnight,*
trying to cool herself down.

The IV bag's electric Kool-Aid,
the phosphorescent surface of Mars.
Rip the bag open and pour the tincture
into champagne flutes, it will taste
like rusty enamel boiled with barley soup.

In time researchers may learn that the roots of hair
can be made to weep but not to laugh. Meanwhile,
she writes her ars poetica in cherry ink on the rapidly
moving water of an Arctic river. Red letter days,
she calls them. Someday soon a widow will distill

a powerful restorative from the weeds
that overrun a burned-out forest. Afternoon light
pours through seven red glass votive lamps,
tiny tea candles within unlit.

TARPAULIN

Betty Goodwin, "Voyage," 2000
oil stick, steel, tarpaulin, rope and oil paint
61 cm x 168 cm x 41 cm
Oakville Galleries, 13 March – 6 June 2010

That old long-distance trucker, Charon,
has driven his transport across the continent
millions of times; used and reused the canvas,
torn and stitched, tied, folded and unfolded,
scraped and frayed and mended it, pulled
metal grommets away from its corners.
The artist has blackened it, rolled it onto a steel ledge –
dark metal altar, mantel height, to hold each one of us.
Four dangling ropes, ends retwined,
re-bound: journey complete. Mummified within,
face turned to the wall, dry hand, bare foot –
awakening old dreams, my mother before
she died: wrapped in a carpet, smothering,
carried out of her house. Raw scratchy cylinder,
skin against bristles, so inhospitable a fabric.

PENNY FARTHING

The grey stone building stands far back
from the road. Massive wooden doors,
high-ceilinged terrazzo halls,
Joe waiting for us in white shirt and tie,
large lean frame and the family face –

strong jaw, straight nose,
crinkling blue eyes and a blitz of white hair.
Pleased with his new socks and slippers.
I saw a white ool, he says, and the ool
flew six times over the house

and three wise men from the east rose up and said
Joe, somethin' strange is gonna happen you –
I went away in a boat at a terrible speed altogether
over the wather like a razor to Canada and Arabia
and I fell in got wet all over stayed in there for hours

until a plane flew down and lifted me straight out
of the wather took me to Toronto and Greece
and the two queens spoke to me.
He nods at my cousin and me.
Senility, we used to call it.

I've heard that ool. I've seen that ool.
When Joe dies Irish relatives send his obituary:
the first person in Ireland to own a penny farthing
bicycle, a bone-shaker, a difficult, dangerous,
accident-prone machine.

CANVAS & SCRAP WOOD, SAWDUST & SOIL, BEDFRAME & CHAIR

Fondacio Antoni Tàpies, Barcelona, Spain

In case you forget, Tàpies peels
your father's handprints off the chapel wall,
illumines his X-rays warped and melted,
whether from anger or affection, you'll never know. In case
you misremember your mother, he pastes a white telegram
to the underside of her table,
lumps of glue on her knives,
knotted napkins a semaphore.
Your father's infirmities, your mother's linens –
hems pierced, holes torn in corners.
Ties your orphan bundle and soaks your memories.

The artist presses his vertebrae through canvas skin,
imprints the curve of his back –
giving life to *arte povera*, the world's
poor material.
                    In the lid of a box his mouth, open
for laughter. Takes needle and thread to
constellate stitches, a failed
and beautiful net. Unties rope,
unfolds what transports – not trucking canvas
like Betty's, but sailcloth.
Not vests, but trousers.

Soundless his violin against a metal shutter –
its strings excised to bind sandbags.

At the moment
of formation or deformation, says the docent.
A six-toed foot. Matter in the form of:
stone, sponge, bed, each
with some small flaw.
The rough *alfombra* where you
place your morning's first real step.
Look at the painted rug, not your feet.
Bite small rips into it, fray its edges.

Gaze cast down, he counts and names
our daily objects. Even a hook on the wall
mirrors the arc of his closed eyelids. This city's
dark years in bricked cellars,
its locations and methods and results,
the innocent bedspring turned electrical.
In case you forget the words *assassin*,
slashes, shocks, bruises.

But see that crown of thorns?
                                    You turn away –
terrible suitcase of religious images.

He takes apart paintbrushes, pries off
their metal casings, scatters bristles
into wet paint.
                    From every country,
every language, he copies the graffiti sign
of the erect penis. A torso sketched
on a mounded pubis of wrapping paper.

He dips your clothes
in glue, lets them meet his
in a mess on a simple wooden chair –
but it's your sweat that hardens them
through the night.

Afterwards, outside, white-trunked plane trees
canopy their foliage over streaming
boulevards. Above it all
his enormous cloud of steel wire,
hovering.

SILVER LEAF

Her former lover said God's anatomy was granite,
        God an enormous Muskoka boulder pierced with veins

of crystal quartz, silver linings we persist in looking for
        and are not always denied – like the surprise

that opened out in her fifth decade when she had given up
        on linings and love

*

She deposits silver into her account: sage, Dusty Miller,
        Lambs' Ears, and the long-fingered

leaves of the eucalypt, beautiful in the downunder but invasive
        when transplanted. The fragrant Russian olive

in the parking lot at the end of her street, the undersides
        of its leaves tarnished by rain.

For her leaf-coins, she gathers tiny orange purses,
        Chinese Lanterns that blossomed one summer

and by the following spring had spread their underground
        rhizomes throughout, each lantern a papery calyx

fading into filigree mantle, a single red berry ripening within.
        Above them, the ever-abundant pear tree

so thickly blooming that its branches seem to enter
        her bedroom, entangling the ferocious dream animals

just as now the wisteria creeps and entwines the wire
        diamonds in the municipal fence.

FURTHER AND FURTHER WEST

HALFWAY TO SOLSTICE

Lotus-filled mooncake month, equinox
about to pry autumn open.
Orangeness starting to gleam in the fields.
Persephone can't find pomegranates,
reseeds the ground with corn.

But among the season's pleasures, we find
splinters and thorns, sudden losses –
the Irish poet who crossed back and forth
on the Giant's Causeway, the one
who felt "babyish" when slowed in his sixties
by a stroke – "I wanted my daddy," he said.

At the small-town farmers' market
we pay for scones and red onions,
remembering the bread queues targeted
by the military in a wounded country.
While we wait at the concession road, a flatbed truck
hauls its cargo through the intersection – drowned car,

an inch of Ontario mud covering glass,
metal and upholstery. *What happened?*
A skid and veer, a slow immersion?
Any passengers? Who rushed to help?
At the tipping point, who did the driver
call out for? We're all in danger,
a lake, a market, a country full
of people wanting solace, wanting rescue.

FURTHER AND FURTHER WEST

My mother had waded well out into dementia,
let's say up to her hips, maybe even her waist.
Her sister similarly afflicted, though maybe just
ankle deep. They were both heading for the island,

the one in the middle of the lake. My cousin told me
she'd taken my aunt to Ireland, and as they were driving
further and further west, they saw the road sign for Innisfree.
I told my mother the story – how my aunt read the name

then recited the poem to its very last line. I began,
I will arise now, and my mother rose to the challenge –
completing the poem, all twelve lines. Nodded
at the end. There, sister. There, horseman. Pass by.

beadwork; or, she re-strings her mother's fake pearls

each Sunday she unfolds
tattered sailcloth
mould stench   lifting off the canvas
winding cloths
drenched history
which ocean less culpable
which less degraded?

*

an African-American poet speaks of
the Black Atlantic
I have had some problems with the Atlantic
human cargo
shipwrecks   the arrival
more hellish than the journey
decade after decade

How men do use their lives
When they try a larger fortune

blanket box
railway spike
treaty vellum
hansard
internment camp
cup of fish broth
moratorium
a continent's web of pipelines

items & moments & mapwork   buried   drowned   overruled

*

1800s, at the Pacific's edge
              Massett beach blued with spilled glass ornaments
          trunkfuls scooped out
              for bison &   sea otter   furs   argillite & tusks

                              *

              she takes out
          that cobalt strand, large cubes of amber
              beads still desert-etched   red Kenyan soil
years ago she intended

              to unstring & wash & re-string
                  they lie coiled in a basket
worldwide trade in beads

                  millefiore Murano
      blown Venetian glass
              slipping from
          her lover's neck in a parking lot in Labrador (she thinks)

when under the weather
              she wants to use her mother's words *I am fed up*
                                          to the back teeth
          she picks up the necklace
              (clear plastic sealer peeling off the imitation pearls
          her mother's)
      & recalls the cord of foxes' teeth
                  sewn onto the cap of the adolescent boy
          in a shallow Paleolithic grave

near Moscow
his hands folded over his pelvis
250 canine teeth of the polar fox sewn onto his belt
4,000 clay beads looped over his body
5,000 for his female companion
her hands similarly folded
anthropologists calculate
45 minutes per clay jewel   so 3,500 (female
non-mechanical
prehistoric) hours
approximately thirty-two thousand years ago

SCORCHED DRESS

Photography exhibit
A Japanese Book, by Ishiuchi Miyako, 2008

On display sixty years later, the clothes
of an ordinary woman whose eyes were drawn
to the bright blue and red flowered blouse,
pattern still vibrant, its puffed sleeves
and matching covered buttons.

A toddler's onesie, whiteness greyed
by the years. Reddish-brown stains
on a schoolgirl's sailor blouse. A dark
gauzy underslip, its left sleeve scorched,
in fragments. Bunched-up gathers of a pink
full skirt. A melted perfume bottle,
an iridescent watch. Two cloth slippers. Eyelet trim
around the collar and cuffs of a girl's print dress.
A black silk chemise with a burn hole in the back.

Like the X-ray prints of bodies on pavement,
the charred silhouettes on the gallery wall.
A Veronica's veil lifted away, portrait
of clothes' endurance, the lightness of all.
The white glove ceremony – unwrapping
and rewrapping in acid-free paper,
immaculate boxes.

PREY

Los Parronales, Chile

1.

The lapwings' cries – a flock of them quarrelling
at my window – sent me out at sunrise for a walk
down the dusty road. Stopped past the vineyard
by an owl just above my shoulder
in an overhanging eucalyptus branch,
a baby rabbit, limp and bloodless,
pinned by the owl's talons to the branch
beneath him. Soft glove-sized grey.
I ran back to the house, gathered witnesses. The owl
remained immobile, unyielding, as we pestered him
with zoom lenses and pity for his prey.

2.

Displayed in his ocean house, all the things
Neruda had captured from the sea. His desktop
washed in by waves. Japanese glass buoys.
Shells from every ocean in the world. A hundred clear
and coloured bottles shaped as men's heads,
another hundred as female bodies.
Bottled ships, bottled sand paintings, bottled
crucifixes. And Wilhemina, the ship's prow figurehead
with her moonstone nipples,
nipples I longed to press my palms against.
But in room after room I was allowed to touch
only the railings on the steep stairs, the wood-pegged floor
beneath my feet. In the open air the wave's spray
and the cutting sharpness of the cove's sand between my toes.

ON READING LORCA'S *POET IN NEW YORK*

Lorca, like you, in my early thirties I travelled
to another teeming and seemingly ordered continent.
Singers in silk garments, coins and the instruments of death
were always close at hand; jailed miscreants,
banners pardoning them,
a deep impenetrable language,
the toes of the tall Buddha, sparrows
sheltered behind his long earlobes. Like you,

I could taste the art and aching everywhere,
I poured the night into black brushstrokes.
The river had not yet been poisoned.
In our hundreds we cycled lampless through the nights.
Lorca, it was not a Wall Street crash but the aftermath
of a decade's rage that splintered
the library's glass cases of butterfly wings and separated
dancers from their jazz. But the iron rice bowl
still sated us and cicada medicine cured us.
The blur of night traffic had not yet killed
my friend on the capital city's ring road.
On every tongue, denunciation and praise. Lorca,
remember how astonishment tasted?

LITANY FOR A VACATION

> . . . outside the circuitry of routine
> you too are vacant, a happy "o" the world
> flows in and out of . . .
> – John Steffler, "Vacation"

O motel of terrible art, highway of fog, of driving
rain; O poison ivy and hiking trail besieged by black flies;
O broken-down ferry, our missed
connection a spark to frayed emotion; flat tire,
garage twenty towns away; expensive cell phone
whose reach exceeds its grasp; O misplaced passport and
pinching shoes; 24-hour restaurant of slow service and
bad breakfasts; O wretched camera
dropped into salt water –
shrink yourselves
into a dozen tiny gnats that we can bat away.

O unexpected fireworks in the summer sky; O thin blue
strip of ocean greeting us at the top of the steep road;
snow crab dinners, a picnic lunch on the rocky hill
so like my family's Galway or Donegal; black whale fluke
with a brief white splash; O stony beach we fell
back upon as we fled the incoming tide's roar; new
and plentiful dreams in wide beds,
O slow lovemaking in the convent-now-an-inn;
O highway of dissipating fog – flare tender
like the soft memory of bites we carry home behind our ears.

PATIO LUNCH

The Minister of Finance walked onto the patio.
Beside us the lake gleamed.
Tiny waves, each a curl of light.
I had been reading about Austria in the 1930s.
I wasn't 100% sure it was the Minister.
I had always thought he belonged in a 1940s gangster movie.
Pleased to do his mobster boss's bidding.
The man in the suit strolled past the tables, looking for someone.
Though he didn't find his party, he seemed self-satisfied and beaming.
My eyes followed him everywhere.
The man went inside to wait beside the "Please wait to be seated" sign.
Lakeside, a clear September sky.
My friend returned from the parking meter and I forgot about the
     Minister.
I began thinking about money.
The consequences of monetary decisions.
Sailboats in the distance, the yacht club across the lake.
Once again the man in the navy suit strolled out onto the patio.
This time accompanied by a beautiful young woman.
Much taller than him.
I said to my friend, That man looks like the Minister of Finance.
She said, That is the Minister of Finance.
I had also been reading about Ireland after the 2008 crash.
No one noticed as the hostess seated the man and the woman.
I remembered the meetings where the Minister scolded the world's
     countries, especially the ones with severe economic problems.
The Minister was smiling broadly at his lunch companion.
He was speaking a bit loudly, mentioning "The House of Commons."
The waitress brought glasses of wine and beer to their table.
I had been reading about riots in Greece and the 30% cuts to pensions.
Foreign aid, military expenditures, calamitous insolvencies in the Euro zone.
The elimination of the penny.
Beside us broken flecks of light jiggled across the lake's surface.

TADDLE CREEK

The neighbours maintain
a normal appearance – BBQ,
camper van, hockey sticks,
noisome leaf blowers.
But there is marital discord
on one side of the street and not the other.
Which is the side that attends
to anniversaries and eavestroughs,
lilac and vinca, which is the side
that dwells in allegory and remorse?
Back and forth the bicycles float;
skateboards clatter over the vertigo.
Underground the buried creek
uncovers bricked-over windows,
rots their wooden frames,
floods our cellars.
Remembering the swans, searching
for a sylvan rescue, we pilgrim to the banks
of the creek, kneel beside its twenty visible
metres, sunshined and then
re-swallowed under Davenport Road.

RUNNING WATER

We'll run water all through the house.
We won't call it flooding.
It will be called work.
Clean work.
Up and down, pipes in every direction.
Horizontal poses more of a problem than you'd think.
Rivers do this effortlessly.
Today in Indonesia and the Gaspé people are swimming away from
    their homes.

The tea making, hibiscus growing, the dishwashing, floor soaping,
    icecube freezing, toilet flushing, all these will stop.
We will run water through the house.
Muddy water.
Fish swim into dragnets.
Mangrove swamps are disappearing, their hold on us loosened.
Rice seedlings are unmoored, tugged away.

Yes, that gold cufflink will be lost, the single memento from your
    great-grandfather.
Also your sweater, handknit in Newfoundland.
You can slip radio batteries into a plastic bag.
Your eyes will sting as you swim away.
You can rest on someone's roof.

This may not happen in warm weather.

We rely on the weakness of the sun at critical times.
Watercolour painting, bean steaming, morning showers and bath oils
    richly scented, percolation and pressure cooking will cease.
We'll sacrifice our cufflinks and carpets, oysters and codfish, our fog
    meadows and ice floes, recall how the Inca studied the Pleiades,
    the seven sisters' storehouse of rain in the sky.

RAIN-SOAKED POEM

after Lorine Niedecker

Dear Lorine, all week I've been thinking
of your cabin's yearly flooding, you
writing from *the other side of a thin door.*
The springtime waters you settled against
with your poetic pump, your ear on
the deluge in your lakeside life. We try to decree
where water belongs, where fire belongs,
but still we drown and burn, railway
capsules of death explode, glaciers
melt, oil streams into the Gulf,
flames devour the café.

                    Lorine, do you recall
how Semele asked Jupiter to show her
his power? He tried to warn her: it
would destroy everything, destroy her.
Heedless, we need to be shown
but the showing ruins all.

Rain in blackened sheets
                draws a basement pond.

Can't we just stand in north woods among birch,
can't we be satisfied with the river-carpet,
shelter on the stone floor of a hollowed-out cave?
Instead we settle a city on a massive
floodplain. That night, up to our ankles
in cold water, we bailed,
ripped carpet and underpadding into strips,
tied them into dripping bundles to send
to the dump. Record rainfall, Lorine,
without even a *delicate pump* like yours
to nurse through the night.

FULL LONG NIGHT MOON

Choppy, we thought, on the ferry crossing from the city
to the Island. December night, a hem of saffron
lining the horizon. But in the Island's outer harbour,
waves crashed oceanic, vociferous against the retaining wall –
like Neruda's Pacific waves, the height of three goddesses.
I saw the whole universe become fluid, felt the elements shift
from breath to roar, warmth to sear, solid to quake.
Consolation to destruction.

When we turned back on the boardwalk: the untethering
of the moon above the skyline, how quickly it rose, looming,
dipped in a mixture of red African sand, turmeric, beaten gold,
a blazing disc, scribbling orange across the waves all the way
to our feet. These colours, where did they come from –
surely not just the sun's brief loan of flame, but that trace,
that reminder of the earthcore's fire and magma.

NUIT BLANCHE

> build you a house out of all this stuff – make bricks
> from all these straws – or failing that, rayon stockings
> – Philip Whalen, "Life and Art"

I'll circle you a ferris wheel we can spin by hand
multicoloured lightclock   through the night

web you a hammock to sling between
                              clocktower & escarpment
to catch
        the hours as they fall

hammer a lifesize music box for you   let its claptrappery music
cuckoo at odd moments
                        I'll supply the words
you the errant tune

sculpt you a marble steering wheel
                        for an onyx car that will never ever
                                                    crash

I'll red carpet you to our front door
                        swing a velvet rope
                                            right into the bedroom

for your festival clothes   patchwork you
                an enormous hooped skirt of ultramarine silks
& rose-petalled satin
                shot through with neon threads

weave you a pair of black net stockings
                stitch a filigreed palimpsest
                                        onto cowboy boots

go striding
                arm in arm with you

NOTES

Listening to the Grass

The epigraph is from Louise Glück's poem, "Pastoral," *A Village Life*, Farrar, Strauss and Giroux, 2006. With thanks to Barry Dempster for the inspiration.

Conditions at the Surface

This poem is for Barbara Sherwood Lollar. The phrase "swift strange prayers" is from "Stage Directions," Lorine Niedecker, in *Lorine Niedecker: Collected Works*, Ed. Jenny Penberthy, University of California Press, 2004, p. 35. Except for phrases in French, italicized phrases are from Ivan Semeniuk, Science Reporter, *The Globe and Mail*, "Reservoir under Canadian Shield may be half as old as Earth itself," Thursday 16 May, 2013, p. A9.

the effect is blue, not periwinkle

is a line from Lorine Niedecker's, "Progression IV", in *Collected*, p. 28.

earthquake

"complex of occasions" is a phrase in Charles Olson's "Maximus to Gloucester, Letter 27 [withheld]," in *The Maximus Poems: Charles Olson*, Ed. George F. Butterick, University of California Press, 1984, p. 184. On Hotspring Island in Haida Gwaii, water flow and thermal activity at the hot springs was stopped by a 7.7 magnitude earthquake in October 2012. Since then, some thermal activity has resumed in Gwaii Haanas National Park Reserve.

Gesture

responds to dancer Nova Bhattacharya's "Calm Abiding," Ipsita Nova Dance Projects, choreographed by José Navas, part of the Kalanidhi Festival of Contemporary Choreography in Indian Dance, Harbourfront Centre, Toronto, 16 March, 2011.

Humming

"the splits of the moon," "into the basin of morning," are phrases
borrowed from Charles Olson's "Celestial Evening, October 1967,"
Maximus, p. 573.

Tortoiseshell

The epigraph is from Charles Wright, "Wrong Notes," *Scar Tissue*,
New York: Farrar, Strauss and Giroux, 2007.

Mailbox

This poem is in memory of Michael Gasster.

Policeman

"What'r you doing in that dress, / a policeman said" are lines from
Lorine Niedecker's poem, "Depression Years," *Collected*, p. 115.

Gweedore, 1830s (Bonfire)

The inventory was researched and recorded by Nuala O'Faolain, in
My Dream of You, Riverhead Books, a division of Putnam Penguin,
2001, p. 103.

Overtime in the Scriptorium

The poem's title is a line by Anne Waldman from "Matriot Acts,
Act 8" in *The Iovis Trilogy: Colors in the Mechanism of Concealment*,
The Coffee House Press, 2011.

Plaza de Puerto de Moros

The line "moving the parts of the body without sound" is from
Lorine Niedecker's poem, "As praiseworthy," *Collected*, p. 223.

Poem Called 'Grateful'

responds to Joanne Kyger's poem, "Grateful," *About Now: Collected
Poems*, National Poetry Foundation, 2007, p. 645.

Adar

borrows from the line, "A Prayer, to the Lord, cast down like a good old Catholic, / on the floor of San Vitale, next to Dante's tomb" from Charles Olson's "Further Completion of Plat," *Maximus*, p. 213.

Quipu

Display note, Museum of Precolumbian Art, Santiago, Chile: "The Tawantinsuyo, or Inca, empire ruled over the territory from Ecuador down to central Chile. The complexity of the Cuzco government and tax obligations produced a bureaucratic functionary called a *quipucamayoc*, an expert in using the *quipu*, the Inca recording system. Inca accountants were privileged employees, but they were not the only ones to use these instruments. Colonial chronicles mention a *quilcacamayoc*, who managed a quipu with different coloured yarns. Unlike the quipucamayoc, these specialists recorded events, stories, and poetry with their knots. They were the empire's historical memory and their *quipus* were learned and inherited according to a family line of descent."

These Persons

The quote is based on a line from Charles Olson's "for Robert Duncan, who understands what's going on – written because of him March 17, 1961," *Maximus*, p. 208.

Valparaiso and Prey

Both poems re-visit "La Sebastiana" in Valparaiso, one of Pablo Neruda's three homes; Valparaiso is an imagined history of that city.

Cormorant Elegy

This poem is in memory of Lina Chartrand.

Wing On

The line "a cross-stitched border of spruce and juniper" is from "Used Handkerchiefs 5¢," *James Schuyler: Collected Poems*, The Noonday Press, Farrar Strauss and Giroux, 1995, p. 99.

Redhead

With thanks to Shannon Maguire for the audio file, and for her "Ornothographies" online workshop in experimental feminist translation.

après vous

After the talk, "Is Ethics Masochism? Or, Infinite Ethical Responsibility and Finite Human Capacity," by Donna Orange, Toronto, 7 February, 2014.

Mothwing

The phrase "mothwing eyebrows" is from James Schuyler's "A Few Days," *Collected*, p. 373.

Cueva de Pileta

"How does the impulse to draw something begin?" is a question on the front cover of John Berger's *Bento's Sketchbook*, Verso Books, 2011.

Rattle

This poem owes a large debt to Lowell Jaeger's "Trash," posted on *Rattle: Poetry for the 21st Century*, 28 January, 2013. http://www.rattle. com/poetry/trash-by-lowell-jaeger/

Further and Further West

The poem makes reference to the epitaph on William Butler Yeats's tombstone: Cast a cold eye / On life, on death. / Horseman, pass by!

beadwork; or, she re-strings her mother's fake pearls

"I have had some problems with the Atlantic" is attributed to Lucille Clifton by Aldon Lynn Nielson in a review of Paul Gilroy's *Modernity and Double Consciousness*, Harvard University Press, 1995; Gilroy uses the term "The Black Atlantic." "How men do use" is from Charles Olson's "Letter 14," *Maximus*, p 63. "Try a larger fortune" is from Shakespeare, *Antony & Cleopatra*, Act II, Sc 6, 34. The information about the Paleolithic adolescents is from David Lewis-Williams, *The Mind in the Cave*, Thames and Hudson, 2009.

Litany for a Vacation

The epigraph is from John Steffler's poem, "Vacation," in *Helix: New and Selected Poems*, Véhicule Press, 2002.

Rain-soaked Poem

"the other side of a thin door / in the flood" is from "some float off…," Niedecker, *Collected*, p. 208. "stand / in north woods / among birch" is from "I visit the graves," Niedecker, p. 210, and is repeated in her "Traces of Living Things," p. 242.

Full Long Night Moon

The December full moon is called the Full Long Night Moon.

Nuit Blanche.

The epigraph is from Philip Whalen, "Life and Art," in *The Collected Poems of Philip Whalen*, Ed. Michael Rothenberg, Wesleyan University Press, 2007, p. 198. Along with so many others in this book, this poem is for Ruth Kazdan.

ACKNOWLEDGEMENTS

"The Poison Colour" was longlisted for *Best Canadian Poetry 2011*. Ed. Priscila Uppal, Series Editor Molly Peacock. Toronto: Tightrope Books, 2012.

"Cueva de Pileta" was longlisted for the CBC Canada Writes Poetry Award, 2013.

"Stone Sonnet" received Honourable Mention in *The Fiddlehead's* 23rd Annual Contest, 2014.

✻

Thanks to the editors of the following journals and anthologies for printing these poems in earlier versions:

Canadian Poetries: "Overtime in the Scriptorium," "Policeman" and "Plaza de Puerto de Moros," online 3 September 2014 at http://www.canadianpoetries.com/poetries/2014/9/2/maureen-hynes-three-poems

Cry Uncle. Eds. Allan Briesmaster, Sue Chenette and Maureen Hynes. Toronto: Aeolus Press, 2013: "Penny Farthing."

Descant: "Small Containers," which appeared as "My Own Veins."

The Antigonish Review: "Nuit Blanche," "On Reading Lorca's *Poet in New York.*"

The Dalhousie Review: "Ars Poetica, Film Noir Version."

The Fiddlehead: "Elemental," "Kindly Stops."

Literary Review of Canada: "The Poison Colour," "Jewel Beetle Dress," "Mailbox."

The Malahat Review: "Further and Further West," "Wing On."

The New Quarterly: "Ply," "Restoration."

Poemimage, Steven McCabe's website, 22 May 2014, http://poemimage.wordpress.com/2014/05/22/rattle-by-maureen-hynes: "Rattle." I am grateful for the beautiful pieces of art Steven produced in response to this poem.

Poems from Planet Earth. Ed. Yvonne Blomer. Vancouver Island, BC: Leaf Press, 2013: "Full Long Night Moon."

Prairie Fire: "Litany to a Vacation."

Queen's Quarterly: "Quipu," "Gweedore, 1840s (Bonfire)."

White Wall Review: "Poem Called Grateful."

Women and Environments International: "Running Water."

To Beth Follett, steadfast and brilliant editor and publisher of Pedlar Press, sincerest thanks for her vision, her care and support.

Special thanks, for inspiration and craft, to Barry Dempster for his workshop in Chile and for years of encouragement; to Gerry Shikatani for sharing the depth of his knowledge in his "Lorca's Granada" retreat, and to the participants; to Sue Chenette and Jim Johnstone for close reading and comments on earlier versions of this book. To Ronna Bloom, Fiona Lam, Ruth Roach Pierson and Jane Springer – heaping thanks for responses to individual poems and years of support.

So many poetry communities have sustained me. For our early start and continuing friendship, the Misses Vickies; to the magnificent Thursday group of Barry Dempster, Jim Nason, Maureen Scott Harris and Liz Ukrainetz; to my Grenadier writing sisters Pramila Aggarwal, Ann Irwin and Jean Unda; to all the members of the Inconvenient Writing Group and the Victoria University group, especially John Reibetanz; to Hoa Nguyen and the merry participants in her classes; and to the fearless and far-flung feminist poets in the Electronic Garret, especially Tanis MacDonald.

My work has benefitted enormously from the extraordinary gifts of Joanne Page's friendship and art, and from her spirit.

And finally, what a pleasure to dedicate another book to my partner, Ruth Kazdan, with thanks for daily joy and endless encouragement.

✳

Vivek Shraya

Maureen Hynes's first book of poetry, *Rough Skin* (Wolsak & Wynn), won the League of Canadian Poets' Gerald Lampert Award. Subsequent collections are *Harm's Way* (Brick) and *Marrow, Willow* (Pedlar, 2011). She is a winner of the Petra Kenney Poetry Prize (London, England), and her poems have been selected and longlisted for *Best Canadian Poems in English 2010* and *2011*. With colleagues, Hynes leads labour history walking tours of Toronto and is involved with "River Poetry Walks," focusing on Toronto's rivers and buried creeks. She is poetry editor for *Our Times* magazine. www.maureenhynes.com